How To Start A Small Business In 2020

The Ultimate Guide to Make You Expert In Starting a Refutable Business Online Or Offline...

Blurb

I want to thank and congratulate you for downloading the book, *"How to start A Small Business in 2020: The Ultimate Guide to Make You Expert In Starting a Refutable Business Online Or Offline."*

This amazing all-in-one eBook by Peter Quac for small businesses is jammed with warm-hearted and tough-minded practices, covering every aspect of growing or starting a reputable small business. The book gives you very useful tips, tools, techniques and fundamental strategies that will assist you in making the right amount of money via the small business. It offers practical strategies used by successful investors around the globe and which are both current and exciting. Thanks again for downloading this book. I hope you enjoy it!

Table of Contents

Introduction

A business is a system of production, distribution, and consumption of goods and services while an entrepreneur is one who can effectively organize the system of production, distribution, and consumption of goods and services. Every business starts with a decision..

The major secret of getting money is solving a problem e.g. the doctors get paid for solving health problems, the mechanic, gets paid for fixing your car, an employee gets paid at the end of the month for solving a part of a organizations problem. What problems are you solving today? You must look for a problem around you to solve. The kind of problem you solve determines the type of money you get.

Deciding to start a small business can be one of the most exhilarating decisions you make in your life. We are living in a world wherever everyone wants to make extra money and add to his income. Most people have achieved this by acquiring great business ideas. When one starts up a company, he must be ready to meet competition. It is important to note that you would not need to become rich or popular to succeed in business but have to think smartly. But there are a lot of moving parts and many different elements to consider.

Chapter 1: Offline Businesses

Compelling Reasons Why You Should Learn How to Start a Small Business In 2020

Small businesses are spreading widely around the world and have now become extremely popular as the most wanted business to start for several reasons. Contemplate for a few minutes what it will be like to work from home and never worry about waiting in heavy traffic jams or to be at your boss call. Maybe now is the time to learn how to start a small business. Wouldn't that be tremendous? In today's fast-moving world, a bit of extra income doesn't hurt, that allows the regular person to get ahead in life so they can enjoy the little extra's life provides, that their existing job doesn't enable them to do.

I'm going to cover with you the 9 best reasons why you should learn "how to start a small business" in 2020 and the benefits behind each of them. I promise once you study them you'll recognize that your 'Small Business' might be worthwhile considering.

1. Work for yourself.

Have you ever dreamed of being your own boss? Well, learning "how to start a small business" is a step in the right direction and the outstanding part is, you'll never have to follow anyone else's screaming orders. You're your own boss.

2. Freedom to do what you want, when you want to.

By being your own boss and with the ability to plan your own work hours, you now have the freedom to enjoy what you want, when you want to and with whom you wish at any time. It's liberating to be in control of your own life and do what you dream about when you want to.

3. Work when you choose to...

This is probably one of the best reasons in my opinion for learning "how to start a small business" because you get to set your schedule for what hours you wish to work. This is particularly beneficial for stay at home mums or dads who have children to attend to and require some versatility in their work schedules.

4. Job security worries are a thing of the past.

By having you own "Small Business" you never have to concern yourself with receiving a "pink slip" from your boss or a "SORRY", but the company has to reduce its employee numbers and you happen to be among the ones who have to go.

5. It doesn't put pressure on your existing job.

You better believe it, you don't have to quit your current job to get started. You can start on a part-time basis until you're in a position to replace your current income by using the income you generate from your new small business. Remember, you are able to set your own working hours for when you wish to work on your business.

6. It builds a "feel-good factor".

Wouldn't it be great to be able to tell all your pals and relatives or just anybody you meet that you're an entrepreneur and you now run and manage your own flourishing 'Small Business'? Pride can also work as a motivator. The more successful a person gets the harder they'll want to work just to achieve the further goals they will have set for the business.

7. Cash is a powerful motivator.

Cold hard cash is a pretty understandable reason for running a 'Small Business'. Why would you start an enterprise if you weren't planning on making any MONEY? It also builds a feeling of security for your standard of living and the things you enjoy doing because the facts is... nothing is free of charge. Everything has a price.

8. You will get a confidence boost.

By setting up and starting your own business venture you will become a more confident person since it takes confidence to start something when you have no idea what the outcome will be as well as what risks are involved, whether or not they are financial or personal.

9. The business could become your retirement package.

If the business turns out to be a SUCCESS and you invest wisely, it would be a great retirement package for you.

Now, take a paper and pencil and jot down why you'd most likely want to learn "How to Start a Small Business", I"m sure you will match a number of the reasons above with me. Having said that, there's a further thing I would like to mention and that is if you're seriously talking to friends and family about how to start a small business, whether it be on the internet or high street, ensure you put together a "Step-By-Step" business plan with all the actions you will need to take and you should definitely start with a business you will enjoy running.

Business Plans For Small Businesses

Writing and developing a business plan is an integral part of the process in launching a successful company. Even if your financing is already secured or you will be providing the seed investment for your endeavor, a written and well-articulated plan can be very beneficial in your quest for success.

The reason for this lies in the fact that writing a detailed plan requires you to review many questions you may have failed to consider. Most plans begin with mission states that articulate the goal, or service, or products your company will offer. They also give a sense of what or how you will distinguish yourself from your competitors. Mission statements can often be somewhat nebulous and I would strongly encourage the aspiring business owner to use it as a way of detailing what their operation will be about. Pie in the sky statements may serve corporate America well, but the real world of most owners is far different. A small company must know what course they plan to chart and what components are required to achieve this.

One recommendation to consider is dividing your plan into two components. The first part should a summary and focus on the general aspects and goals your company will seek to accomplish. The second and much lengthier portion should focus on as detailed aspects of how to run your day to day operations. Of course, forecasting the financial future and specific scenarios is very difficult if not impossible. We need only look at weather forecasts to see how difficult this endeavor is. Nevertheless, the exercise of going through each major component of your business should be done.

Another major component is the marketing strategy that will be followed. Since advertising and marketing are the key mechanisms for securing sales, this should be a very detailed section. In fact, taking the time to call radio stations, newspapers, or reviewing pay per click campaigns and the projected costs involved is worthwhile. One of the difficulties small operations face is not taking into account or underestimating the amount which marketing campaigns will run. Underestimating these cost s can be costly and can threaten to leave your hard work unrewarded.

Most plans also include a management section covering how your new enterprise will be supervised. Many entrepreneurs fall into the trap of managing on the fly instead of determining what their role will be and how they will resolve their time to adequately work in the business as well as take the time to step back and review the big picture from time to time. Doing so can alleviate or even prevent headaches in the future.

Why Is Vision So Important To Your Small Business!

What are you trying to achieve? Where are you going? What do you want your small business to look like in 5 years? Answer these questions and your day to day decision making will change...

A small business vision can be compared to planning a holiday! People usually decide where they want to go for holiday based on the offerings of the destination. If it's a relaxing holiday they are after, they may go to Fiji. But if it's for shopping, then Dubai may be their choice. If it's to climb the Sydney Harbour Bridge then they will go to Sydney, Australia. Holiday destinations are determined by desires, with a few restrictions like budget and time available.

The same should apply to your small business. In 5 years time, what do you want your small business to look and feel like?

- ❖ Do you want a large street frontage or small office at home?

- ❖ Do you want to be actively involved or have a manager controlling your employees?

- ❖ How many employees do you want?

- ❖ Do you want a business with excellent cash flow or a business that is worth a large sum of money when sold?

Answers to these questions and much more will help to provide a clear vision of your small business in 5 years time. And often, this will completely shape your growth. The majority of small business owners start a small business based on their trade or what they know. They never usually give much thought to their small business vision. While it's comforting running a small business using the skills you have, sometimes this can be a recipe for disaster. A business should be kept simple and always be fun. But business owners tend to make a simple thing into a complicated thing and let others control them.

Owning a small business should mean a better lifestyle - flexible and shorter working hours and more money. But this is hardly ever the case; it's more like working 60+ hours a week for about $4 an hour.

Why is this so?

Because small business owners have never sat down and thought about their vision. They don't know where they are heading, they have nothing to aim for. They have no idea what the finished product will look like, so the business eventually takes control.

Decisions are based on what happened that day, instead of the business vision you are working towards.

Take the time now and think of your small business vision.

❖ What will your small business look like in 5 years?

- Why should your customers remain loyal to your small business?

- How will you beat your competitors?

- What will make your small business attractive to any buyers?

- What are all the potential risks?

Think carefully about these questions and then write your vision down. This will immediately tell you, the universe and anybody else, exactly what you are creating. It gives you a defined target to aim for and achieve.

Business Ideas For Small Business

Before you can become a successful Entrepreneur, you need a good business idea. A good business idea is a very subjective thing, as different people with different personalities can make different ideas work. In general, when you are first brainstorming ideas, no business idea is a bad thing. Your goal is to eliminate business ideas by running each idea you come up with through a feasibility self-assessment analysis and eliminating the ones that are not that good ideas for your particular situation. When you have done that, you should be left with a core list of good ideas that you can sit down and think about. Ultimately, business ideas can be divided into categories of goods-based and service-based, with those categories being further subdivided into online and offline endeavors.

Goods-Based, Online

When you consider goods-based services that are predominantly online services, several websites come to mind. For example, any website on ClickBank, Commission Junction or any other affiliate hub would be websites that are online and goods-based, because they all happen to sell a product of some kind. The advantage of this website is that you can create the product yourself (i.e. the e-book website) and therefore save a lot of money in start-up costs. The disadvantage is that promoting it can be somewhat difficult, especially if you want to do it for free.

Service-Based, Online

There are many services that you can provide online. These include offering online writing services to people that need web content, creating websites for people that don't know how to do it themselves and administering websites for people that are looking for that kind of help. You can create an online business around some sort of online service and then branch out and start looking for clients. This is a lot harder to do from an effort point of view, but the big advantage is that it costs you practically nothing.

Goods-Based, Offline

Goods-based companies offline are about as easy to recognize as they are in their online form. Any shop that you visit when you need to purchase something is an offline shop that is based around the sale of goods. The supermarket, the department store, and the convenience store are all examples of an offline business that is primarily based around goods.

Service-Based, Offline

Contractors, for the most part, can be considered service-based. These are people that will paint your house, clean your floors and renovate the areas of your house whenever you need it. These are editors that will work on your manuscript and they are also personal trainers that will ensure that you get the workout you need. These are all examples of services that can be done offline.

Combination

One of the best things about starting a business in the modern world is that you can combine these things in order to create larger business ideas. For example, you can do online writing and you can also edit manuscripts offline. This would allow you to work at building up a writing business from two sides and that ultimately would be very good for you in the long run. But remember in order to run a truly successful business it first pays to have a solid business plan.

Project Management for Small Business

Large business and Government have been using project management for years as a way to deliver critical business outcomes. But project management is not just for the big end of town. Small business can also benefit by using project management tools and techniques to drive the achievement of their objectives.

What is a project?

A project is defined as "A temporary endeavor undertaken to create a unique product or service". A project, like a business, requires the use of scarce resources to achieve a predetermined set of objectives. Large or small, most organizations now refer to key actions, activities or tasks as 'a project'.

But what is project management all about and how does it apply to small business?

Project management has to do with the management of a project. It requires the identification and management of several key elements. You need to determine:

- ❖ What you need to do (the scope)
- ❖ Why you are doing it (the mandate)
- ❖ How it will be achieved (the approach)

- ❖ When are resources - human or otherwise - required

- ❖ Who will perform each task (resourcing)

- ❖ What can go wrong (risk management)

More specifically you need to ask the following questions:

Why

- Why are you doing the project?

What (Scope)

- What are your objectives?

- What are the tangible and measurable outcomes you are trying to achieve?

- What are you not doing?

- What are you not sure about?

How (The Plan)

- What is your approach - ie how will you deliver the project?

- What resources do you need?

- What is your budget?

- What are the tasks to be done?

- What are the deliverables - ie what is produced?

- Are we going to have regular meetings to discuss the project?

When (Schedule)

- In what order to things need to happen - Are there any dependencies between these tasks - How many people are required at what time?

Who (Resources)

- Who will work on each task?
- What is their workload for the project as well as their other activities
- Do they know what they need to do and the timeframes to do it
- What Can go Wrong (Risk Management) - What are the show stoppers?
- What are the predicable problems?
- What is the impact if any of these occur?
- What can we put in place to minimize any impact?

The Project Manager's Role

Once you have determined the project scope, budget, resource requirements, and schedule and identify the potential show stoppers and risks, you need to appoint a project manager to drive the project forward.

- The project manager plays a critical role. They are required to:
- Manage and lead the project team

- Communicate and negotiate with the project team and the rest of the organization

- Make decisions

- Plan, monitor and control work performed by the team

- Report on progress

- The project manager needs to be given sufficient authority to 'crack on' with the job at hand and provided with the resources to ensure the project will be a success, and not bet doomed to failure from the start.

Common Pitfalls

Through experience, there can be several challenges that many organizations face when attempting to manage critical projects.

1.   Some things just take time - Many individuals and organizations fall into the trapoccasionally of specifying 'magic dates', they will arbitrarily set dates that are unrealistic. Suddenly they're surprised when the target dates are not met. Plan activities using realistic timeframes taking into account the available resources. Wishing and hoping and are not valid scheduling techniques!

2.   Focus on outcomes, not activity - Projects are all about achieving an outcome, notrunning around and been busy. Identify and plan activities based on the outcomes they achieve or the deliverables (documents, systems, etc) they will produce. If you are performing a

task that does not produce a deliverable that contributes to the outcome the project aims to achieve, you are doing something wrong.

3.   Don't just meet for meeting sake - Meetings are more than an opportunity to talkabout the weekend or your favorite football team. All meetings should have a purpose, an agenda with all action items being allocated and set a target date.

4.   Failing to plan is planning to fail - Despite popular opinion, planning anddocumentation are critical to ensuring a successful outcome. As much as 75% of the project schedule may be spent on planning and design in technology projects. Plan the project from the start. One the plan has been established, then work to the plan.

5.   Projects run late one day at a time - Whilst a day here or there may not seem like a lot,they all add up. Many organizations do not focus on ensuring all critical project deliverables are delivered on time, with the net result being the 'oh-my-God' moment when there is the sudden realization that the project has run off the rails. Once late, projects very rarely get back on track.

In summary, Project management is not complex, difficult or too hard. Effective project management requires the application of a systematic and disciplined approach. It is through this focus, businesses of all sizes can utilize project management skills, tools and techniques to drive critical business outcomes.

Six (6) Keys to Success in Setting Up Your Small Business

Often when we arrive at that decision to start our own business it is with that intent to pocket a few extra dollars for ourselves and family. But just having a great idea is not enough. There are a few key ingredients that go into ensuring success in your small business. These are examined below; 1) Be passionate about what you are doing.

Even if you are not fully knowledgeable about what you are doing, your passion will likely get you over the bar. Your knowledge will increase. Where your heart goes your body will follow so a little passion and enthusiasm will go a long way to ensuring your success.

2) Set achievable goals and work towards them.

The most critical aspect of your successes and achievements is your ability to measure them. Unless you have set goals how will you know if you are growing? Every entrepreneur needs to have a long-term vision for where he wants his/her business to go. Tied to that long-term vision is a series of smaller goals. This is what holds your business together on upon which your success is built. Motivation is a key benefit that manifests itself in your accomplishments and as you go from victory to victory you will continue to build momentum and snowball into a pillar of entrepreneurial success. This is what tells you that you are doing things right.

3) Humble yourself, be willing to learn

One of the biggest mistakes you can make is to go about your business with a "know it all" attitude. Be open-minded and seek counsel where necessary. Read, network and submit yourself to forums or interest groups in your field. As you do you might be surprised that new ideas take root because of this kind of exposure. Be willing to share your experiences and knowledge and others will reciprocate in like manner. Don't be too concerned about competing with your colleagues. Just do what you know is right and you will get your just rewards.

4) Learn from the mistakes of others, you don't have to repeat them all over again.

I can guarantee that you will make some mistakes of your own at some stage in your new venture regardless of how knowledgeable you are, and you may have to pay for them. What is certain also is that some have already been made for you. You won't have to pay for those. You must get as much information as you can about what you are doing. Do your research, ask questions and learn. Almost anything you can think of as a viable business idea has been thought of already. What happens after is what you need to be concerned with. Did the venture fail? Why? Certainly, you don't want to make that same mistake again. How successful is it, and what is the most profitable line? How long have they been in operation? This does not mean you will go out there and mirror what the other guy is doing but at least you will get a good appreciation and insight in terms of the direction you should or should not be heading.

5) Don't try to reinvent the wheel.

Learn from the mistakes of others but learn from their victories also and capitalize on them. Do not go out trying to recreate what has already been done. Some situations will debunk this notion, especially where copyright infringement and such are concerned. But if you are looking for quality images for your site, for example, you certainly don't have to go snap them yourself there are enough resources online you can choose from. You may have to pay a small fee in some cases but you will have to weigh the pros and cons before making your decision. In the end, you may very well find it save you some valuable time and money.

6) Be patient !

Time is the one currency that has to be spent to ensure success at whatever you do. It is inevitable and we all know this. But we sometimes get ahead of ourselves in expecting unreasonable results in little time. We need to curb our enthusiasm otherwise we can end up frustrating ourselves. Everything takes time and in business, this is no different. While we need to continue to be positive we have to set reasonable goals and be patient as we grow and achieve them.

The Challenges You Must Overcome to Turn Your Small Business Into a Big Business

You might have a small business today, but you don't want that label for the life of your business. When entrepreneurs make endeavors, they are looking to create a business that will rule the world one day. However, every business has to face some struggles in the beginning that it must overcome to become big business. The way you handle these challenges decides the fate of your small business. Today, you will read about these challenges and the solutions to them, so if you are a small business, you can set the foundation for its success.

1. Knowing the Target Market

One of the biggest issues with most small businesses is that they don't know their exact target market. Sometimes, they don't know how to narrow down to the target market. This is a huge issue because you could have a perfect product, but you might pitch it to the people who don't need it. Keep in mind that people who don't need your product won't buy it even if you try to give it to them for free. On the other hand, people who need your product will be willing to buy it even if it is priced high. For your business to survive, it needs to start selling as quickly as possible, and that's why it is important to find your target market before launching your product.

Solution :

The first step of identifying your target market is to know your product well enough. You have to ask yourself some important questions about the product and write the answers down. For example, you have to ask yourself "what existing problem does my product solve?" You also have to know if there are any other solutions available in the market for the same problem. If yes then you have to see how your product is better than them or how you can make it better. Conduct surveys on the street and social media to know the personas of the best buyers of your product.

2. The Right Type of Marketing

Businesses, small and big, have huge parts of their budgets allocated only for marketing purposes. However, modern technological advancements have proven that a big marketing budget does not translate to successful marketing. So, you might have done a great job in identifying your target market, but if you approach them in the wrong way or through the wrong channel, you will not be able to reap any benefits from even the most potential market for your product or service.

Solution :

Identifying your target market should help you identify your marketing methods and channels too. For example, if your product is for people aged over 50, you would not want to make Instagram the prioritized marketing channel because only 18% of the users on Instagram are aged above 50. Similarly, any product that targets executives, marketing officers and professional people should be promoted on LinkedIn before any other platform. After knowing the buyer personas, you should also select the type of marketing that best suits your potential audience. If you are creating a hip-hop music video for marketing to retired individuals or an opera video for 18-year olds, you are doing it wrong. Use website analytical tools to know what appeals or does not appeal to your website, visitors. Base your digital marketing campaigns on data-this is the era of data-driven marketing.

3. The Funding Problem

If there were no funding problem, every person who thinks of a unique idea would have a business. In the real world, funding is always a problem, and it is exactly the point where the journey ends for many aspiring people in the business. However, it is not always the lack of funds that kill many small businesses before they even start. The important part is how much dedication you show in arranging those funds. Sometimes, people have the options available, but they do not knock on all the doors.

Solution :

First, you have to know all the options you have available for arranging the funds. If you are not okay with arranging funds through the bank or in the form of a loan, take a look around at your family and relatives. You will be surprised to know how many of the people in your circle will be ready not only to give you the investment you need but become a part of the endeavor. The crowdfunding options are also there. You don't even have to go to the investors personally today as you can visit a platform like funded.com and arrange funds online.

4. The Right Leadership

You can't make a business successful unless you have the right leader in place. It is not completely untrue that the attitude of the leader sets the attitude of the rest of the employees at a company. If you lack confidence in your leadership, you will end up hiring people who lack confidence in themselves. One of the biggest problems with most small business owners is that they can't convince themselves to delegate responsibilities. They believe in their skill so much that their mind never accepts that someone else can handle the responsibilities too. They end up taking the responsibility of everything on their shoulders and mismanaging things at the end of the day.

Solution :

The first thing that needs to be fixed here is how you think. If you find it hard to delegate responsibilities, get rid of this habit as soon as possible. You can't handle everything as the business grows and so you have to create a team right from day one. Do not hire people just because they can do the job-hire people who share the same vision as you. Do not settle for good employees because finding the best ones is taking time. Do not try to take matters into your hands all the times. Listen to everyone that's part of the team and the decision making process. Have a great relationship with your employees.

5. Setting the Price

One of the most difficult decisions for a small business owner is to set the price of his service or product. When you are a small business, you can't afford to have a full-fledged marketing department. Of course, when you have a marketing department, they can set the price of your products, but when there is no marketing department, you are the one to take this decision. Price too low, and you might not make any profit at all. Price too high, and customers might never buy your product.

Solution :

It will be tremendously helpful in this scenario to take a look at your competitors and how they have priced their products. Secondly, you have to know a simple rule to set the prices of your products and services. You first set the price to cover your costs. Once you have started covering your costs, you set the price to cover the costs and make a profit. Once you have done that successfully, you start adding your "value" to the price. You should also know the buying power of your target market so you can keep the price within their comfort zone.

These points cover pretty much every big challenge that a small business comes across. Keep in mind that some of the challenges might be exclusive to your business and industry too, but if you can overcome these common challenges, you can cover the industry-specific difficulties as well.

Time Management Tips For Small Business Owners

Most business owners already know that 20 percent of their product comprises 80 percent of their sales. Save time in the long run by discovering exactly which products or services are driving the business. Focus the majority of your energy on the important things and cut back on the time you devote to the other 80 percent.

1. Learn to prioritize

Just as 20 percent of your product drives your business, some of your activities are more productive than others. It is an old but good time management tip to tackle your most important projects first. Teach this strategy to your employees so that you will all find the time to complete the important projects. Once you rank your activities based on the order of importance, give yourself a set amount of time to complete them. For example, give yourself a time limit to return phone calls and reply to emails, and try not to go over it. Sticking to some sort of a schedule will help you stay focused on important projects rather than get lost in the mundane activities that do not drive your business forward.

2. Make a "to do list" every day

You may think that you do not have the time to write a list every morning. However, it is easy to become overwhelmed by the sheer volume of chores that face a small business owner each day. Last minute interruptions and distractions can make the most focused business owner forget to finish a task. A brief but thoughtfully prepared "to do list" will remind you of what you need to do that day. This will prevent you from forgetting to call back your important client. Do not go beyond the day's work when writing the list, and set reasonable goals. Getting ahead is great, but you can work on that when the list is finished.

There comes a point in every business when the owner must learn to say "no." Whether you are dealing with a needy employee or a difficult customer, spreading yourself too thin is not good for your business. Yes, you need to make customers happy, but sometimes they will ask for the nearly impossible. Consider whether or not doing something is good for your business before saying yes, and learn to delegate.

It is tempting for small business owners to waste their time micromanaging every aspect of their company. However, some tasks do not require the presence of the owner. Teach employees to take action and make decisions within the boundaries of their positions. This is extremely difficult for the micromanager, but it does provide you with time and energy to focus on other more important activities, such as bringing in more customers. Should an employee call you about purchasing equipment? Yes. Should an employee call you because someone was two minutes late to work? Probably not. Creating parameters that define the extent of each employee's decision-making authority will keep a small business owner from having to put out minor fires. Having clear boundaries will also build up employee morale. In all honesty, people generally hate being micromanaged. You hired your employees for their talent, so why not put it to good use?

4. Communicate with your employees and be aware of your business' deadlines

Small business owners are still in charge, and they need to communicate with their employees to ensure that they are on the same page. Discuss the deadlines with them each week and make sure that they contact you with any new developments. Stay connected to your clients and try to prevent any miscommunication that will affect projects late in the game.

5. Be sure to take some time for yourself

This feels counterproductive. Many company executives and small business owners are guilty of confusing busy with productive. However, human beings need time to rest and decompress. Numerous studies have shown that taking short breaks improves overall productivity. The brain is not wired to work nonstop. People who take breaks make fewer mistakes and work faster. A study by Dr. Coker explains that people who take short breaks online are nine percent more productive than their overly stressed colleagues. So relax a minute for the good of the company.

6. Stay focused on your goals

What do you want from your business? Set aside sometime each month to examine your goals and how you are getting there. Look at what strategies are moving you forward and identify which ones are dragging you back. This might sound easy, but many small business owners are so focused on the day-to-day activities that they put off examining their goals regularly. However, constant evaluation can save you time and money as you discover which methods work for you.

7. It is tempting to try to save money by doing everything in the house

However, outsourcing is often more cost effective than doing everything yourself. For example, the time that you take working as an accountant could be better spent following up leads and building relationships. When 35 percent of small business owners lament not having the time to grow their businesses, it is clear that small business owners are taking on too many mundane tasks.

Outsourcing specialized projects not only frees business owners to work more effectively, but it can also benefit the company's image and profitability. For example, hiring a graphic designer to create a brochure will probably yield better results than simply typing something into a Word document. If you really cannot afford to outsource a project to a professional, look inside the business. Chances are that you have a multitalented staff. Someone with an interest in graphic design might to a better job than you could, and this individual just might be willing to work a little cheaper than a professional would, for the experience.

8. Staying busy is not growing a business

Every business owner needs to evaluate his or her schedule. Yes, a responsible owner knows what is going on and will have to put in quite a few hours. But are the hours being spent most productively? How much time do you spend putting out fires and running in place? Your time is valuable, and you must use it wisely to move forward. Some of the time management tips explained above might seem counterintuitive or expensive, but consider the loss your business faces when you cannot find the time to be with your customers. A business owner is the face of his or her company. People buy from owners they trust. But, if the owner is never seen, how can customers get to know him or her? Landing a sale will probably more than compensate for the $10 an hour you pay for an outsourced employee. Learn to use your time wisely and expand your business while you improve your quality of life.

Steps to Starting a Small Business - Important Things to Do In Putting Up Your Business

Starting your own business may not be easy but once you have the right ideas in place and you have prepared well, starting up may not be that difficult as what you think. If you are thinking of putting up a small business, brainstorming on the small business ideas might be one of the first things that you need to do.

If you are eager to put up your own business, it is also important to be able to familiarize the different steps to starting a small business. Here are a few things that you should not forget if you are trying to put up a business and you want to start right.

- Brainstorm and think of a business that is right for you. You have to consider your skills, your knowledge about the business, the profitability of your business in the location you want to put it. One of the most important consideration also in choosing a business is the demand for the product or the services in a particular area that you want to cater to.

- Make sure you have a comprehensive business plan for your business. A business should start with a plan to guide you through the important details of starting it up. Your business plan should contain your objectives, how you can achieve your objectives and business goals, as well as the financial and technical aspect of running the business.

- Have market research. If you think you can just skip market research because you are only putting up a small business, you may be wrong. Whether you are putting up a large or small business, business starters need to know their audiences. This will help you decide on what are the current demands of your target market and the services or products you can offer.

- Have the necessary training that can help you put up your business. Of course, you have to be knowledgeable enough about the business if you want to succeed with it. Get assistance if you need as well. You don't have to do everything by yourself. Even if you are putting up a small business, it does not mean you have to go through all the business by yourself.

- Decide on the type of business that you want to put up. You can go into business alone as the sole proprietor or go into a partnership. Of course, there are different advantages and disadvantages of both and weighing up the pros and cons can help you decide on which way to go. Among the considerations, you have to make is the money capital available as well as profit sharing.

- Process the necessary papers, licensing as well as registration of your business.

- These are just a few of the steps to starting a small business. Do your homework and research on everything you need to know in putting up your own business so you will also be able to assure that you are making the right thing right from the start.

How to Finance Your Small Business

If you have a great business idea or plan, or you would like to expand your existing business, don't let a lack of funds stop you in your tracks. There is a wide variety of financing available for small businesses. Let's take a look at the financing opportunities that small business entrepreneurs can take advantage of.

While the financing sources comprise diverse institutions, such as banks, government sources, venture capitalist and "angel" investors, it is useful to look at what all lenders, regardless of category, want when they loan money or invest in a business enterprise.

When you seek money for an already existing business, lenders will be interested to know about the history of your business; whether it has a track record of good management and good performance. Lenders will be keen to know whether you can repay a loan and will look at your present cash-flow to see whether it is sufficient to enable you to meet your current obligations as well as to take on extra debt.

Your credit history will also be under scrutiny. Good credit history will help you to get a loan. If you have had problems in the past, it is best to bring these to the attention of the lender yourself and explain how you have turned the situation around.

You can also bolster your chances of getting a loan by putting up collateral. This reduces the risk for the bank in case you default. And finally, if you can show that your money is invested in your enterprise then lenders will have more confidence in the proposition.

Many small business loans are turned down due to poorly presented proposals, inadequate collateral, insufficient cash flow and a lack of management experience.

These are the general points that lenders and investors are interested in, now let's look at the main sources for small business financing.

1. Traditional Lenders: Banks, credit unions, and finance companies are the main source of loans to small businesses. Many of these institutions have a small-business department and are experienced in handling small-business loans. The most logical place to start is with the institution which handles your business and personal banking. You should do your best to get to know the manager and personnel at the bank. So don't try to save time at the ATM! Being friendly with the bank staff will not guarantee you a loan but it will make it easier for you to make your loan presentation.

2. Government Sources, the Small Business Administration (SBA): The
programs of the SBA work in conjunction with the traditional lenders, as they are mostly loan guarantee programs that reduce the risk to lenders in case of

default. Some of the popular SBA programs are as follows

a. *The 7(a) loan guarantee program:* This program helps businesses which lack sufficient collateral, by providing repayment guarantees ranging from 75-85% depending on the size of the loan.

b. *The SBA LowDoc loan program:* There is only one form to fill out for these loans and approval time is rapid (within 36 hours from when the SBA receives the applications. These loans are only for amounts up to $15,000 but they can be used for start-up businesses.

c. *The SBAExpress loan program:* This is another quick-procedure loan guarantee program, but it covers loans up to $250,000. The SBA guarantees 50% of these loans, and interest rates in this program may be higher than in the other SBA programs

d. *Microloans:* These are loans for amounts up to $35,000 which are made by nonprofit community-based organizations.

3.   Venture Capitalists: These are typically firms that are seeking investment opportunities in companies with high-profit potential. Usually, when you take money from a Venture Capitalist firm it means that you have to give up some ownership and control to the investors. If you are thinking of going in this direction, then it is imperative to investigate the VC firm and make sure that it has good references.

4.   Angel Investors: These are individual investors who are looking for good opportunities in a wide variety of businesses. You don't have to be a high-tech company to attract these funds. Angels have smaller sums to invest than venture capitalists, and their investments range from $100,000 to $1 Million. There are a good number of angel investors in the U.S. and Canada, with at least 170 investment groups or angel networks spread around both countries. You can find the angels by making a search on the Internet, looking for angel associations in your particular area of business. You can also inquire with your local small business librarian, the chamber of commerce, your local SCORE office and with other non-competitive businesses.

As you can see from this brief survey, the money for small businesses is out there. Prepare your proposal carefully, and approach the institutions or individuals that best match your needs and capacity.

How to Effectively Brand Your Small Business

Branding a small business is a must if you want to succeed in a competitive world. The importance of branding a business disregarding its size is based on not only real benefits, products and services that your business possesses, but also an image concept that all businesses should keep in mind.

From business cards to global business identity, depending on how effectively you brand your business, the more or the fewer opportunities of success will knock at your door. The reason why large companies brand their businesses is that they know this is the best way to differentiate their products and services from their competitors while creating a corporate image.

Many small business owners believe it is not necessary to develop a corporate image, particularly those whose business integrate just a few individuals as staff, or even when they own one-man business, using the internet for selling or promoting their professional services. However, even a small business should utilize the same principles as large enterprises to brand their business.

Furthermore, if your business has business cards, stationary and other branded elements along with a matching website, you will not only create a corporate image, but also loyal relationships with your customers and prospective customers, who will find more reliability with a small business with these characteristics, than others without a professional look and feel.

Because you only have the opportunity to impress new customers once, you should make sure that this impression is a positive and lasting introduction and a handshake, only possible if you brand your business conveniently and professionally. There is no need to spend thousand of dollar to achieve it, but do not go to the other extreme using uneven elements.

Small businesses should be aware of the elements that will make their brand unique and recognizable, including consistency between online and printed elements, such as your logo, signage, business cards and even a slogan that helps people understand at a glance your business's mission statement.

Effective branding must achieve these goals; be consistent and never differing, carrying the same logo, colors, slogans and statements through to every element of your business, all of them always visible and unique, hence the need to avoid elements that anyone can find anywhere such as free or cheap clipart.

Creating your brand, whatever your budget requires a business plan to have a solid appreciation on whom your customers will be and what can you do to serve them. This is not only a matter of elegant stationary or catchy business cards; it is the most important deployment of a small business for an eventual growth in future terms.

Marketing Your Business Offline

Every marketer is searching for the most effective ways to promote their business online. But, how about offline promotion? The answer to that is really up to you. Remember, all your customers live in the physical world and can be reached more effectively from the physical world. With that being said, regarding promoting your business offline you must start thinking creatively.

The following are just a few examples of various marketing techniques that can be used.

1.   Create business cards. This can be done with business card paper which can bepurchased at business supply stores. You can make these on your home computer. You will need to install card-maker software to do this. Or you can hire someone to make them for you. Try to make them unique, different than the normal business card. Be creative, try and capture the attention of prospective customers with your choice of color and design.

2.   Pass your cards out at dinner engagements, parties, libraries, schools, colleges,daycare centers, any place where someone will allow this type of solicitation. Leave them in restrooms of theaters, restaurants, department stores, etc. Remember, think creatively and you will come up with tons of other places and ideas.

Keep a fresh supply of your business cards in your car at all times. You never know when an opportunity will present itself.

3.	Make up some flyers and posters to post on bulletin boards. Again your choice ofcolor and design will be substantial at capturing the attention of prospective buyers. These flyers could be handed out locally and also posters could be displayed at various locations such as supermarkets, gas stations, malls, laundry mats, churches, social clubs, and business centers.

4.	Talk to your friends and people you come in contact with about your business. Thesefriends and acquaintances will tell their friends and so on. This is called "word of mouth" advertising. "Word of mouth" is by far the most effective marketing technique you can use when promoting your business offline. Be enthusiastic about your business while you're talking, get excited about what you do. Your enthusiasm will most likely rub off and result in sales and/or recruits.

5.	Place bumper stickers on your car displaying your business. Include a phone numberor a website link so that people can see it and contact you. You would be surprised at how many people look at these. Again, you can make them yourself or hire someone to do it. For this technique, your website URL and phone number should be fairly large so that it can be seen easily.

6.	Hire someone to make ink pens and pencils with the name of your business on them.You can leave these at banks, churches, libraries, and various other places. When you start to hand these out, you will most likely think of a lot of other places to hand them out, or discretely leave them.

7.   Check out cinema screen advertising at various theaters. Think of how many peoplewill see your ad! The prices will vary. This is an excellent marketing method if pricing is within your budget.

8.   Check out advertising in your local newspaper. Advertising in magazines is alsoanother great option. Many people are newspaper and magazine junkies. If the pricing is within your budget...go for it!

9.   Have t-shirts or hats made with a special logo of your business? Include a phonenumber or website link to your business. Other personal favorites could be mugs, calendars, mouse pads, refrigerator magnets and the like. And I bet if you think real hard, you could come up with a lot more. Creativity is key when contemplating innovative offline marketing techniques. Offline promotion is a trial and error type of thing. If something is not bringing in the sales...try something else. The ideas are essentially endless. Put your mind to it and try your hand at offline promotion...it could mean significant success for your business.

Top 8 Mistakes Small Business Owners Make

When starting a small business most entrepreneurs are full of enthusiasm and high expectations, but around 50 % of them fail within the first five years. Reasons for the failure are diverse and numerous, just like the risks involved in starting and running a small business. Here are some tips on how to be within that 50 % of small businesses which manage to sustain and succeed.

1)   Jump straight into a new business, dive in headfirst: Realistic and objective relationship with your own business starts when you start your company. Sometimes there is no time to analyze and think too much, unplanned opportunity shows, it is the right moment, etc. But mostly you do have enough space to take a critical look at your venture before investing too much time or money. Think about things such as the weakest part of your plan, competition, chances on the market, what would you do if this plan wouldn't work. These critical analyses will help you avoid some of the basic and very common mistakes. Believe it or not many of them could be skipped at the very beginning.

2)   Underestimating how long it will take until the business starts to supportitself and you: This simply means two things. First-you must be aware that each new business needs a lot of time to spread and start functioning-earning money, and you must count with that-being prepare to see no income for a first few months. Second-you must calculate how much exactly it is going to cost and what period is necessary for your business to attract regular customers/clients. This is the most serious mistake and problem which make people bankrupt and give up.

3)   Not knowing your customers: When you get an original idea of your business, your next thought should be the market and the customers. No matter what kind of products or services you provide, you must know in the first place what is your target group of people, who are your potential customers, what do they need, how can you help them, how can you reach them. And even when you already have a solid customer base, you must be careful about changes in fashion, finances, approach, and everything that come with the times which are changing.

4)   Spending or borrowing too much: Initial high expectations can work against small business owners when they lead to borrowing too much. When you take a credit or a loan from the bank, don't forget that you are the one who is going to return that money and your business won't start generating profit immediately. The larger the loan, the larger the monthly payment. When you do get the money for your new company, be careful of what you are going to spend it on. Don't spend too much on equipment, furniture, hiring too many employees and renting a huge space. Go step by step.

5)   Not being prepared for taxes: If this is your first small business to run, you must remember the taxes, as the regular monthly cost. People often make this serious mistake thinking only about invested money and profit it will bring. But you have to fulfill a couple of obligations to the state, you can't avoid them and these amounts are not low, especially if you let them accumulate. It's a good idea to have a separate bank account only for this purpose, put money into it from each payment you receive.

6)   Lack of marketing and advertising plan: A marketing plan is a part of your initial small business plan. It creates the kind of attention you want to get in front of your customers. It is what attracts people to you and it is a story which stands behind your products or services. That story is what people like to buy. Especially if your business is fresh new, marketing is the only way to let people know you are there. Having a website, a good website is a good way to promote your business and make it visible.

7)   Ignoring the employees is a mistake many entrepreneurs make: You might be the key to everything but you cannot do everything. That is why you hire people to work for you (the right staff). By "right" I mean people who know their job and do it well. And for that, you have to make them feel useful, important and respected. If you share your ideas, success, and money with them, you will get positive feedback, and that will have a positive impact on your company.

8)   Giving Up: As we have already said building a business isn't an instant product. It is a very reason many companies shut down so soon. But, if you have control over your finances and realistic business plan you should never give up when you come across the first obstacles. All the good and important things require a certain period and having in mind all the challenges of running a business brings, it's normal that the beginning is hard and not each period of the year is equally successful. If you're not starting then keep in mind all the bad moments you used to face with and how did you face with them. Some of the most successful entrepreneurs failed a few times before doing extremely well.

Trading As One of the Best Small Business Idea

Trading is one of the best business idea because once mastered, it can be duplicated over and over again. How will my trading strategies benefit your quest for making money? You will have a mathematical edge using these strategies.

Trading will no longer be emotional it will just be following rules. It will show you how succeeding is about controlling risk and maximizing profits! There are three types of trading. Day trading, swing trading, and position trading. All three have their advantages. What they all have in common unlike traditional investing that most people are used to is a plan.

When most people invest they just park their money and hope the market goes up. They have no clue when they will protect against losses and even worse when they will take profits. There are two ways to analyze entering and exiting positions. They are referred to as technical and fundamental. Technical analysis is the key to making consistent profits.

Technical Analysis

Many people want to learn what is referred to as the art of making money. If you can predict market direction, you can make some serious money. Technical analysis is a huge part of making money as a trader. It's basically like a language and some people speak it and others don't. If you know how to speak the "language of technical analysis" you can be a very successful trader. The reason I say "can be a successful trader" is because there are other aspects of trading that must be learned to be successful, various strategies and position sizing just to name a few. If you learn technical analysis you will know when to get in and out of your positions.

Of course, you will be wrong sometimes about your entries and exits that why you need to learn how to control risk by using stop losses and hedging techniques. If you learn technical analysis and combine it with option strategies; you will make a lot of money! If however, you don't learn technical analysis, you won't know when to get in and out of positions; this is more or less like shooting in the dark. The reason technical analysis works is simple. By looking at a chart you're looking at the human activity. The reason is prices move up and down because humans are buying and selling something. All of these humans are looking at the same chart as they buy and sell a certain stock.

People have very powerful emotions while they're trading stocks. By looking at a chart, technical analysts can tell at what prices will the stock most likely go up or down. By knowing the language of technical analysis you're simply looking for patterns that occur over and over again every day in the market.

If you know patterns that tend to repeat themselves you have the advantage of knowing what will most likely happen to prices next.

None can ever be right about the direction all the time. All successful traders have some kind of edge that allows them to succeed over time and for many of them, technical analysis is their advantage.

Your strategies should all have specific plans behind them. You know exactly when you're going to cut losses and exactly when to take profits before you even get into a trade. It turns a small business idea into a systematic process that produces profits!

Contrary to what you might have been told in the past, the best way to reduce losses and maximize profits is by using options. Options are the backbone of most successful traders. I will prove this to you! Learning how to trade options is the biggest step in making serious money in the markets. I will focus on two types of trading, swing trading and position trading.

Swing Trading

The process of swing trading has become a very popular stock trading strategy used by many traders across the market. This style of trading has proven to be very successful for many committed stocks and Forex traders. Traditionally swing trading has been defined as a more speculative strategy as the positions are traditionally bought and held for the trader's predetermined timeframe. These time frames could range anywhere from two days to a few months. The goal of the swing trader is to identify the trend either up or down and place their trades in the most advantageous position. From there the trader will ride the trend to what they determine as the exhaustion point and sell for a profit. Often swing traders will utilize many different technical indicators that will allow them to have a more advantageous probability when making their trades. Shorterterm traders do not necessarily tend to swing trade as they prefer holding positions throughout the day and exercising them prior to the close of the market. Swing trading strategy utilizes time and it is this time that is the deterrent factor for many day traders. Often there is too much risk involved with the close of the market and that a trader will not be willing to accept this risk.

The distinction of swing trading is a broad topic in that it has many different influences from a multitude of different trading strategies. All of these trading strategies are unique and have their respective risk profiles. Swing trading can be an excellent way for a market participant to further enhance their technical analysis skills while giving them an opportunity to pay more attention to the fundamental side of trading. Many successful swing traders have been known to use a Bollinger band strategy as a tool to assist them in entering and exiting positions. Of course, for a swing trader to be successful at the strategy, they will need to have a high aptitude for determining the current market trend and placing their positions in accordance with that trend. It does a swing trader note good to place a short position with the plan of holding for an extended period of time in a market that is clearly trending upwards. The overall theme here is that the goal of the traders should be to increase their probability of success while limiting or eliminating risk. The swing trader's worst enemy is that of a sideways or in an active market. Sideways price action will stop a swing trader cold in his or her tracks as there is no prevailing trend to key off of.

When used correctly swing trading is an excellent strategy used by many traders across various markets. It is not only used in the Forex market but it is a key tool in futures and equity markets. Swing traders take the skills that they learn through technical analysis and can even parlay these skills into various options strategies. The short-term nature of swing trading sets it apart from that of the traditional investor. Investors tend to have a longer-term time horizon and are not traditionally affected by short-term price fluctuations. As always, one must remember that swing trading is only one strategy and should be utilized only when appropriately understood. Like any trading strategies swing trading can be risky and conservative strategies can turn into day trading strategies quite quickly. If you plan to employ a swing trading strategy, ensure that you fully understand the risks and develop a strategy that will be able to allow you to generate maximum percentage returns on your positions.

Position Trading

Position trading refers to the style of trading in which trades are taken and held for a considerable period of time, anywhere from several days to several months. The majority of long term investors practice this style of trading because of its many benefits. Position traders usually do not bother themselves about fluctuations, which in most cases tend to be short-lived. Investors using this style of trading study long-term time charts such as weekly and monthly charts to identify potential trade opportunities.

When practicing position trading, you are not entering a position in the market and quit it at the end of the trading day. Position trading involves entering a position with a longer time perspective. Position traders aim to identify trade opportunities in financial instruments where the technical trends and/or the fundamental analysis of the instrument imply a large movement in price that is about to take place, but that which may take an extended period of time to yield good returns.

Position trading is a flexible style of trading. Traders can effectively engage in it while retaining their day time jobs. Because they mainly use weekly and monthly charts for analysis, they can take as little as a few minutes every day just to check on the progress of their trades. As such, it is regarded as one of the easiest ways of navigating the financial markets, without having to glare at the computer screen all day long.

Just like in any other style of trading, position trading requires adherence to discipline and keeping to the rules. Importantly, because the "long term" perspective is the backbone of position trading, personality and level of risk tolerance of traders can either work for or against them when practicing this type of trading. In position trading, sometimes a trade can be negative for days or even weeks. However, you should be able to be patient and allow enough time for the decision you made to result in profits.

Nonetheless, this does not mean you should stay in a losing trade if you discover that the decision you made will not work according to your initial expectations.

To start position trading in any financial market, you should have an in-depth knowledge and understanding concerning the macro-economics and associated issues. Keeping an eye on a long term position can be easy; however, identifying a profitable long term opportunity can be something different.

So, I hope this information was useful in developing trading ideas and furthermore a trading plan that works for you.

A Practical Methodology for Mitigating Risk in Your Small Business

The Practical RiskMAP is designed to boil down Risk Management processes into a simple and understandable framework that every business owner can and should apply. Protecting your business the right way shouldn't be an option for anyone serious about their long term success.

Implementing the principles outlined in the Practical RiskMAP is an affordable way to protect your business the way it should be protected. Until now these processes have not been readily available to small and medium-sized businesses in an affordable and practical format.

- Expected Results

At the end of your exploration of the Practical RiskMAP process, you will have taken a very important step in handling a part of your business that frankly a lot of your competitors haven't even addressed.

You will have the basics of a methodology that you can use to handle risk in all aspects of your life. You can continue to educate yourself on these processes and implement the steps yourself or you can utilize available external resources.

- What's This Going to Cost?

The beauty is that even if you utilize external risk resources, it's likely that you can spend less than what you are currently spending on your current insurance program alone. The fact is that many businesses don't allocate their insurance budgets very efficiently because they don't understand that not every risk needs to be insured.

- Be Smart!

Simply ignoring your risk and hoping that those unknown "What ifs" just won't happen isn't a smart business strategy! You've spent countless hours growing your business.
Take a few to make sure you don't get blindsided.

✓ The Practical RiskMAP Process

The Practical RiskMAP process can be broken down into the following steps:

1. Risk Identification

You can't manage something you are not even aware exists. A huge portion of the Risk Management Process is eliminating secondary ignorance. Secondary ignorance is not knowing that you don't know something.

You need to identify as many risks that your business faces as you can. Note, this is constantly changing and might never be complete. You don't necessarily need to become a risk management expert, but you do need to know what resources are available to you.

2. Risk Analysis

Risk Analysis is the process of estimating the potential frequency, severity, and priority of the risks your business is exposed to. If, for example, you evaluate the exposure of an employee getting in a serious at-fault auto accident while driving to a sales call. The frequency of this occurring is (hopefully) low. The severity measured in dollars can be very high.

There are other "human costs" and implications that can arise out of accidents and exposures, but for our purposes, we will measure severity in the financial impact to your company, (and potentially to you as an individual).

3. Risk Control

Risk Control is a process of determining the most economically efficient method of handling the risks your business faces. The word control is a bit of a misnomer because you can never completely control all risks. This step does help you assess which risks you should Avoid, Prevent, and or Reduce.

4. Risk Financing

Risk Financing is determining the optimal financial vehicle to transfer risk. This can transfer the risk via a contract or by securing an insurance policy. In many instances, it makes sense to retain (self insure) the risk. But which ones do you retain and which ones do you transfer?

5. Risk Administration

Risk Administration is the process of implementing and monitoring the program. This is an ongoing process that consists of procedures you implement internally as well as coordinating external resources to help you with loss control.

Risk Tenets

- Don't retain more than you can afford to lose.

- Don't risk a lot for a little.

- Consider the odds.

- Don't treat insurance as a substitute for loss control.

Effective Risk Management Programs utilize at least one risk control and one risk financing technique for each exposure.

How To Compete With Other Small Businesses Ethically

Competition and one's ability to succeed in the face of competition is crucial to a business's success. But oftentimes, a business will employ any measure to ensure that they get a step up over the competition. Often, unethical measures are used such as spying on the competition, slandering them, or bribing customers not to go to a certain business. The competition can indeed be cutthroat, but there are ethical measures one can take to succeed and maintain the business's integrity.

#1: Focus Your Marketing Efforts On What Your Business Does Well, Not What The Competition Is Doing Poorly

It's tempting in your marketing efforts to speak to what the competition is doing wrong or to put down your competition. I believe that the best way to make your business stand out above your competitors is to focus on the things you do best. If you give excellent customer service and always put the customer first, it's best to emphasize that as opposed to saying that your competition doesn't do well in the customer service department. If one inquires as to why your customer service is better than the competition, it is best to speak to what your business does exceptionally well as to customer service and make the point that it's something that makes your business unique. This will help set your business apart from the competition and not set off any ethical alarms.

#2: If Someone Else Is Putting Your Business Down, Resist The Temptation To Fight Back

It's easy not to make insulting comments about another business, but what happens when that business makes insulting comments about yours? It's hard to sit there and do nothing as there is no telling what impact the insults may have on the prospective leads that you are trying to get. Striking back is never the right answer because it starts a back and forth war of words and insults that could lead to disastrous results down the road.

If a rival business makes insulting comments about your business that are true, the best course of action is to address the criticisms and make it clear how you plan to address them. Use the comments as a chance to make changes and improve your business. If a rival business makes insulting comments that are not true, your best course of action is to do nothing and continue. If your current customers are believing the comments, it is best to address that to them personally instead of the business who made the comments.
Always keep cool and keep focus on your business.

Chapter 2: Online Businesses & Passive Income

Why Starting an Internet Business is Your Best Choice Now?

Establishing a small Internet business is much easier than any traditional business. Internet brings equal playfields for anyone who wants to start a small business, home business or simply want to work on an Internet job to earn extra income during spare time-regard as a "part-time job Online".

Do you know what will likely go down as the most colossal, most lucrative goldmine in mankind's' history? It is the Internet. The Internet has become a worldwide revolution, radically changing the way the world communicates and gets its information.

E-commerce and shopping on the World Wide Web is already a multi billion dollar industry... soon to be in the Trillions.

The Internet offers you the best financial opportunity. Anyone with commitment can succeed if they choose the best online businesses, follow a clear marketing plan with good marketing tools.

There are a lot of advantages and benefits for starting online business:

1.   You can start affordable Internet businesses with LITTLE capital and have thepotential to make MILLIONS. Build an income well above what many conventional businesses.

2.   You can build Online business and run it from anywhere in the world. Even when youare on vacation. The only tool you need to carry around is the laptop. If you don't have a laptop, you can use computers in libraries or "Internet Cafes'" to check on your business (assuming your email is accessible remotely).

3.   You can reach millions of visitors if you have websites! How many people visit theMom-and-Pop corner brick and mortar store? You have the global market.

4.   You can start and run your best Internet businesses at home office. You need just asmall room or desk where the computer can sit on and an internet connection from your home. You can reach the world from your home.

5.   You do not need to hire anyone, but yourself. You can earn while you learn. Do not tryto master everything at one time. It will cause frustration. You apply what you learn, and learn from what you've done. Gradually you will master the internet world.
6.   You can do your business in your spare time. You do not need to quit any daytime jobwhen you start your business. It is best for those working moms and dads. You can work when your kids sleep. You can work at any time of the day or night. It is also a good part-

time job opportunity for college students who can apply computer skills and make money for their tuition.

7.   You can let your automatic system do the work for you. Run your business onautopilot

Plus TAX Advantages.

As a home business owner, you can hugely take advantage. You can deduct the cost for your business travel, meals with business partners, and home office costs like your computer, internet connection, telephone, and other tools related to your business.

As you can see that there is a lot of potential from best Internet businesses and the leverage is enormous. Starting your online business should not put you in debt. Hundreds of internet business owners who are making $100,000 more per year started for less than $200! You can be successful with your own business without investing much money, as long as you do the right things.

Take advantage of every free and low-cost resource. Like free trial for 90 days, free bonuses, free eBooks, and more.

All you need for starting your best Internet businesses are the following:

- A good computer

- An internet connection

- Choose best Online businesses

- Build your business and follow a good leader

- Marketing your business with effective marketing resources

Once you find a good online business model, with a good leader's help, and right promotional method, you are on your way to earn a good income online.

How to Begin a Small Business Online - 5 Basic Strategies

Not everyone, business owners or prospects, wants to do extensive market research and read reviews but you need to spend time and effort in the planning stages of your business.

✓ You should know your target market

Before you can begin to market goods or service to the public you should know your target market. You can find useful information about a market niche from suppliers, an interview done by an expert and from "observation" surveys. You should make a list of questions that you want answered and survey a group of business experts or business prospects; you can have this done for free .

You should set-up campaigns to gather potential customers on your marketing list because once you know your target market you can reach them promptly. You can also pay into a marketing list of target customers. You can research online to find marketers who will allow you to promote your products to their customer base. You want to target customer on your marketing list to make money.

✓ Spend time and effort to get things done

You need to schedule a time to work on your online business. You will need to follow through on your hard work and effort; some people will begin today and get frustrated by the next day. You have to maintain a focus on getting to where you want with your business ideas. If you not investing time into your business, you may be missing on some relevant issues.

If you are looking for a long-term business online you have to spend much-needed time with gathering information for your business. If you are beginner, you need to spend time and effort to know more about internet marketing. You will need a guide to succeed online; therefore, you should put out some effort to get relevant contents into your marketing strategy.

✓　　You should promote what people are buying

If you want to make money online you should find a profitable niche market and promote. This may sound too simple but this is how market research comes in handy. Maybe you are new and you cannot provide huge bonuses but you need to add some extra value to be competitive online. If you are selling the same high demand product, there is no reason for you not to make money.

You should present something special about the market that has not yet said or you can get a short report that is related and offer it as a freebie. There are quite a few tricks and tips you might need to improve your marketing. You can enter a few keywords or keyphrases in the search engine to get help with some of your answers. The bottom line is this; you have to promote products people are searching for online.

✓ Finding a profitable niche and make some money

Some of the most profitable topics/niches online are in the make money from home, Health, Wealth, Travel and Life-style businesses. You will have to search online for useful resources and information on your specific niches or micro-niches. You do not have to worry about product creation because research ideas are online to use for any home business. Some stats reports show what markets are profitable.

If you can identify what people are doing or buying online and find a profitable product to advise or help them with their cause, you can make some money. A profitable niche product is generally products people will continue to use for the long-term; through-out their human life-cycle. People who are diagnosed with illness need to recover and if you can choose any product from the list of profitable niches to help them, there are possibilities for you to make money.

✓ You can use an e-commerce website to promote

Your next move now is to find good promoting methods to begin making a business presence online. There are more to just using links to promote. There are proven methods to start promoting online and you shouldn't have to pay much dollars to have a business on the internet.

With a website, you are more flexible to market your business on a wider scale. You can use a website basically to send visitor/traffic while promoting multiple products. To build an e-commerce website used to be an obstacle for beginners wanting to start an online business but this is no more since the easy website builder software and the userfriendly form editor make building a website simple. If you are having any doubt about website design you might want to outsource some of this task.

Once you have develop your online business skills and a level of internet marketing; finding a niche, promoting a product and finding a hungry market will become a routine and you can target any niche market with authority.

5 Mistakes When Starting an Online Business

When first starting an online business, many people make several mistakes. Because of these mistakes, they will quit, give up, and then think online businesses don't work or it's just a scam. Having an online business can work and can be fun if you avoid a few mistakes. Here is a list of 5 mistakes you must avoid.

1.   Jumping from one niche to another. When starting an online business, you need to define a niche market and stick with it until you have profit coming in. Stay focused, even on the hard days. If you have too many niches going, you will not be able to help your customers and you will be stretched to the limit. Once your niche is doing good, you can start a new one and possibly be able to outsource some of your work.

2.   Don't try to do too much! With an online business, you need to take baby steps. There's a lot of information to absorb when learning how to start an online business and if you try to conquer it all right off the bat, you will lose focus and fail. Set minimilestones, not fantasies. For instance, work on a marketting article and once mastered, you then try video marketing, and so on.

3.   Learning from too many people at a time. Pick one or two people to learn from. Take action on what they teach you and once you've mastered that, you can go onto another course, program, or person to teach you. If you learn from many people, you will have information overload and this will freeze you up. You might not know were to start from.

4.   Failure to take online business like a real business. If you don't know where you're going, how will you know when you get there? The importance of setting goals for your online business is huge. Be serious about your business. Set weekly, monthly, and yearly goals. Set a daily schedule for yourself. This way your family and friends will take you seriously and you will know every day when you are working. Setting a timer for each task can help keep you on track.

5.   Focusing on the money when starting an online business can add stressto your life and make your business unenjoyable. Focus on your customer's needs. The money will follow after. When you focus on providing a great service, your customers will be happy and they will keep coming back to you. Be genuine and be yourself, if not, people can't see right through you.

When you avoid these 5 mistakes when starting an online business, it will make your new journey much more enjoyable. Stay focused, set small goals at first, pick genuine people to learn from (there are a lot of people trying to make a quick buck), and most of all...enjoy it!   Remember, anything worth having doesn't come easy, but it's always worth it. And most important of all, take action!

The Best Website Design Plans for Small Business

If you own a small business or wish to take part in online marketing, then you have to design a good and reliable website. There will be a lot of problems if you are a fresher in this field. You really need experience and skills to perform online marketing.

If you are a small business owner also you can have a good website. Many companies are specialized in designing the website for small business owners. They perform so because that will be more interested in the work of different companies they maybe not interested in the money.

Some website developing companies that are also new in the field will perform the works at a very economical rate. They do so to get credibility in the field. They will compromise with the money as they are also fresh. The work in these companies will also be good as they will try to their maximum potential. You will be able to communicate with these companies more than other well-established companies.

There are a lot of advantages to choosing small business website development companies. You will be able to share your ideas and impart your creativity. The professionals in these companies will help you more to design a good strategy for your online business. Search engine optimization is a very competitive field you should have the content and design of the website to facilitate that. Therefore you can choose a company which will provide search engine optimization and website designing.

Outsourcing website design and promotion works are also now very popular. By this, you can save a lot of money as many companies are having less cost of labor. But choose the best company to design and promote your business in the online market.

How To Promote Your Online Business Offline

Do you promote your online business offline?

If you answered "no", then you link most online business owners. We are so engrossed with ways of promoting our websites online that we forget about offline techniques.

If you've not been using offline techniques, then you are missing out on a lot of traffic. Here are a few offline traffic tips you can begin to use today.

1. Word of mouth

Start promoting your website by telling people about it. Tell as many people as possible. If you don't, don't expect others to. Everywhere you go, seminars, workshops, social gatherings and so on, make sure you seize opportunities you get. If you have a gardening website and you find your self in a gathering that is interested in gardening, make sure you refer to your website.

2. Newspaper/Magazine Ads

Regularly place ads promoting your websites in local, national and niche publications. Place small ads at first. If you write quality ads, the small ads will work well.

Make sure your medium of advertising is targeted. When I say targeted, I mean make sure the medium is relevant to your offer. Like promoting dating website in a romance journal.

3. Article writing and distribution

Like article distribution online, this is a technique that works offline as well. Write quality articles related to your niche and submit to the editors of targeted newspapers. Make sure you write an exciting bio box at the end of all your articles. This is what will make the readers want to contact you. You will be seen as an expert.

4. Stickers

Create stickers with the name and logo of your website and stick on your car, door and other places you can. Distribute if freely so that people can paste everywhere. Make your business name a household name in no time.

5. Do everything

Do everything mentioned above and every other legitimate ways you can promote your website. Remember it's your business and it is your responsibility to ensure that it succeeds.

How to Spot a Great Passive Income Opportunity

If you are going to sell something online, or offline, would you like to get paid once, or would you like the idea of getting paid over and over again for the same sale? Remember, most of the time, it takes the same amount of effort to sell a 'one-time commission' offer, as it does to sell an offer that pays a passive residual income every month.

So, when you're looking at creating a passive income online, you need a few things in place, obviously great products or services are essential and yes, you can produce your products, but then you need websites, marketing materials, auto-responders, sales letters, support, etc, etc.

The other alternative and one that is much easier is to find a company that has proven products or services, a sales funnel in place that works and people that are doing it and making money.

Are there passive income opportunities out there that you can join and use all their marketing materials and websites, that have already been tried and tested at a cost of thousands, sometimes millions?

Well, the good news is yes, there are passive income opportunities online, ready and waiting for you to join and tap into their experience and materials that will, if you follow what they say, guarantee success! Remember, these companies have already tried and tested everything, they know it works, you just have to follow their instructions.

Things to look for in a great passive income opportunity:

1. Awesome products or services that you know people need.

2. A blueprint step by step system, that anyone can follow easily.

3. A support system.

4. Make sure the company you are joining is established and successful.

5. The opportunity to earn as much money as your heart desires.

6. They must have up to date marketing materials, especially online as the marketingmethods online, change regularly.

7. You need an opportunity that is continually evolving with the market, do not go withone of the dinosaur companies and there's plenty of them out there!

Very quickly, you can start making a passive income for yourself. But a word of warning, if you're one of these people that are looking for the magic bullet, you know the people, the people who hand over 20 dollars and expect to be millionaires within a month, without doing anything! Then when they are not millionaires they will say they've been conned. The truth is, you are going to have to work very hard, but if you find a great residual income opportunity, they should have a proven, step by step, success blueprint, one that you simply follow and implement.

One of the most important things to remember when you have your own home-based business, the success or failure is down to you, you have to take responsibility and take this business seriously if you do, it's only a matter of time before success happens. You MUST take control and realize that the success or failure of your home-based business, is down to YOU.

Like many people, you will probably start the business on a part-time business because, at first, it's not your main source of income, this is a great idea, but make sure you put aside a regular amount of time each day, to build your business.

Once you have chosen your residual income business opportunity, take responsibility and push forward with unstoppable determination, you WILL see results.

Powerful Means of Increasing Passive Income

Making a passive income is beyond the average person comprehension especially those that work from nine to five. They only know of one way to make money, work a certain number of hours and be rewarded for it proportionately. The rich on the other hand do not work for money, they have their money working for them and making a passive income. They spend their time and effort building systems and empires that will do the work for them. Long after they have built their empires and systems they will continue to receive income for the initial work that they performed. These systems and empires will keep earning them an income for the rest of their lives and beyond to their children's lives. You must learn to work smarter and not necessarily harder if you want to have a passive income. For the average person, this is a completely new approach to making money and creating a lifestyle that will take care of them and their families.

If you want to increase your freedom and independence then you must make a passive income. You must be able to maintain your lifestyle even if you're not working. The person working from nine to five has money concerns if he or she is unable to work and they have very little freedom or independence. Most people are drained emotionally from worrying about their money or the lack of it. Most family problems are in direct relationship to a family not having enough money.

How do you increase passive income in your life? Most people would say that this sounds too good to be true, financial freedom and making an income for the rest of your life. Getting a purpose and being hooked on it is the first step toward a passive income. Once you get a taste of receiving a recurring income month after month you will be hooked and it will encourage you to work on ways to increase your income until financial freedom is within your reach.

Real estate is the most popular way of creating and increasing recurring income. To own property and lease or rent it out you can continue to receive a passive income with only small maintenance expenses. Another way of earning a passive income is to invest large amounts of money and earn a return on your money. Unfortunately, the average person does not have the amount of money needed to make these two systems work for them.

There is another way and that is to be the author, songwriter or play-wright of the year. You could receive a royalty on your book, song or play long after the work is done. The only problem with this method of receiving passive income is that you must be very talented and be willing to work tirelessly.

The alternative solution for the average person looking for an affordable way to receive passive income lies within the realm of the internet. With or without a business or a product you can turn to the internet to create a passive income through affiliate marketing. You can earn a commission on somebody's product that you like and are willing to promote. Large amounts of money is not needed, a minimum amount of time and a basic knowledge of the internet is all that's needed to get started. By going at it gradually you can work your way into financial freedom and a very lucrative recurring income.

The internet is the ideal place for putting systems in place that will keep on bringing in the income for the work that you do once. Almost anything that you set up can be automated to run twenty-four hours a day and it doesn't take all day to set them up. It only takes about a half-hour to set them up and they bring in an income every month.

We can have the financial freedom and independence we desire if we will take the time to get started. The answer for you is out there on the internet and are available to you. You can make the choice to start making a passive income or stay with the nine to five concept. You can choose to work smarter or to work harder. The choice is yours.

Increase your lifestyle for life choose passive income.

Great Ways to Earn Passive Income Online

1)   Blogging: How in the world does a blog make you money? Simple, the power of Traffic. Think of famous bloggers and how they can sustain their lifestyle simply by blogging. The more traffic you bring in, the higher the potential for those visitors to click on an ad and buy something. Advertisers will be willing to pay to work with you as they all know this. This usually comes in the form of either direct advertising or some type of affiliate marketing. To be successful as a blogger, you need to find something interesting to write about, draw an audience, and then keep it coming.

WordPress is a good way to start as they provide a cheap and good platform to start your money-making machine.

2)   Affiliate Marketing: Affiliate marketers often focus on promoting certain products where they get a percentage of the cut if a product or service gets sold.

This can be done either on your blog or niche websites that offer quality content on whatever field you are in. Through the use of dozens of affiliate broker services out there (Google AdSense, Amazon Affiliates, Commission Junction, Flex Offers, Click Bank, etc), they allow you pick from thousands of different products in your particular niche and promote them on your blog or website. When people click on them and buy the product, you get a cut. Of all the passive income ideas, this would fit the idea of "passive" most. Simply because income is generated as people click on your ads, you don't have to do anything at all.

3) **Email Marketing:** This is another form of affiliate marketing where you use your list of blog subscribers to promote a certain product. This is quickly gaining popularity everywhere as it allows people to earn money working from anywhere with enough internet to send an email.

Lots of successful bloggers swear by this process because they claim that your website subscribers are a "target audience" for your niche; thereby increasing the chances of more purchases.

4) **Niche Websites:** Unlike blogging which can be very time consuming, why not make a smaller one focused on one particular topic. These types of websites are called niche sites.

A niche website may be as small as 5 pages (also called a micro-niche site) or as big as 100 pages. It all depends on how much work the creator wants to put into it. Webmasters make money from niche sites either through the advertising or by selling them at auction websites like Flippa.

The successful ones take it to the extreme and create a portfolio of niche sites. Think about it: If you had 10 sites each bringing in an average of $600 per month that would be $6,000 of passive income.

5) **Selling Items on eBay:** Go to antique fairs or estate sales, people have no idea that they may be incredibly under-selling something. Turn it around and sell it for more on eBay. In just a few sales you could potentially double or triple your money.

6)   Drop Shipping: Drop shipping is when someone places an order with you, and someone else (usually a manufacturing company in another country) makes the product inexpensively and ships it directly to the customer.

You never see, handle, or do anything with the physical product other than managing the whole process.

This is very efficient because you as a seller, don't need to have any inventory, overhead costs, storage costs, and very little liability.

7)   Free-Lance Writing: If you like writing blog posts, or just like writing in general about certain topics, you could always sell your services to people who need some good content. You could offer your services on Elance, Freelancer or Fiverr to earn some quick cash. Another place you could score writing deals is at the really popular sites like eHow, About.com, and Yahoo.

Offering to write for bigger blogs and publications can help build up your reputation which will then help you command better and better rates.

8)   eBooks: Do you have an iPad or Kindle? Then you've probably noticed that eBooks are selling like hotcakes and people are willing to spend a few bucks to download ones that seem like they will be worth the read.

If you have good knowledge about a particular topic and love to write, the Internet makes it easy for you to assemble your eBook. One of the nice things about putting an eBook together is that you could leverage the traffic of Amazon to list it and sell it. You could also use other means of marketing such as eBay, ClickBank, or even your blog.

If you have no writing talents, sites are selling the licensing rights (as low as $5.99) for books that are already written so you can rebrand and resell them.

9)   App Creation: Apps are extremely popular right now. Just think flappy birds. Everyone from all age group with a smartphone or tablet knows what an app is and is usually not shy about spending a few dollars to get one or to buy upgrades from it.

Apps are nice because they generally don't require as much programming as a full-scale software suite would take. If you know anything about programming, you could make one yourself.

Or you could outsource the creation of the app to freelance programmers. Apps make great passive income opportunities because all you need to do is list them at a popularly traveled app marketplace such as Google Play, Amazon or Apple.

3 Secrets to Start a Successful Global Business Fast

Why is a global business so important?

A global business creates the ultimate freedom of earning income wherever you go. It also gives you a competitive advantage over businesses that are limited by language and location.

✓ **The Internet as the ideal business platform for a Global Business**

The Internet has grown explosively in the last ten years as it has become more widely available and used. To date, many entrepreneurs, small startups and corporate enterprises have used it as the ideal business platform to grow a worldwide business.

✓ **How is an internet business different from a typical "Brick and Mortar" business?**

Problems of Traditional "Brick and Mortar" Businesses -

1. Convenience: Tangible products require physical delivery and increase the need for added manpower. Recruitment and the expense of additional manpower can be a hefty operating cost. Product shipping and negotiation of

consignment deals with distributors demands a lot of time and patience - Business is a hassle.

2. Costs: Establishing a brick and mortar business in a popular location, easily accessible to customers is costly - The more people the location attracts, the higher the rents! As sales increase, there are costs to produce additional products. Throw in other factors like huge packaging, advertising and employee costs and Business is costly to maintain.

Criteria for a Profitable Global Business -

As computers and technology become more affordable, populations with Internet access are greatly increasing. With it comes the opportunity to extend the reach of your business to these populations.

As recommended by the experts, here are the Top 3 criteria you should consider when starting a profitable global business:

1. You need a multi-lingual business website that attracts daily web traffic

Unlike a traditional business, which is restricted to a limited geographic area, an online business can have customers located around the world. A multi-lingual website allows you to reach all of these people who are potential customers for your internet business, and their numbers are constantly expanding exponentially.

It is also a cheap way to provide global customers with information, instead of catalogs or advertisements that have high development and publication costs. 2. You need a hot selling information product that doesn't need delivery

As opposed to physical products which have production, packaging, storage, and shipping costs, the cost of providing information is primarily in the time spent to create it. An information product removes the need for manufacturing and physical packaging. It is also more convenient for customers to download the information from your website rather than going through the hassle of delivery or shipping it to them.   3. Set up a fully automated business system that runs even while you sleep

Nearly every aspect of an internet business can be automated. Order processing, credit card processing, and electronic delivery can all be automated.

Your business can operate 24 hours a day, 7 days a week, with little or no human intervention required.

Auto responder software, which automatically sends emails to customers, provides an opportunity to remain in contact with customers, and nurture them toward repeat business.

How Global Business Strategy Consulting Can Help Your Business

Since the launched of your small company, you have been faced with stressful days, sleepless nights, and multiple challenges every day. Your business is surviving the tough and unstable economy, yet you wish for it to thrive and prosper even more. You turn to books and magazines for help. You talk to other business owners for advice, guidance, and support. You welcome every opportunity that could help enhance your business. Yet, you have failed to seriously consider looking into international management consulting. You think that this type of investment is only apt for businesses on a larger scale than yours. However, you must know that such an investment can significantly affect yours as well. These consulting firm tap on marketing, sales, and management tactics as part of their global business strategy consulting strategies. This kind of support can prove to be extremely beneficial for your company's success.

When a business owner decides to invest in a global business strategy consulting firm, you make available to you the relevant intervention of a third party who can see the bigger picture, thus being able to better advise you on various aspects relating to your company. International management consulting can help you in setting short and long term goals for your company, formulating strategies, and employing smart and efficient tactics to ensure the achievement of your goals.

As mentioned above, investing in international management consulting firms will make available to you much sound advise about various marketing strategies that can be employed in order to most effectively tap your business' target market. Consulting firms are knowledgeable about various market trends, business approaches, plans, and tactics that could help you in attaining your goals as efficiently as possible. Global business strategy consulting firms will put much effort into ensuring that your company will become an active and aggressive market player in no time. Hand in hand, you can work towards success, longevity, progress, and growth.

International management consulting firms can also be depended on to formulate admirable plans and schemes that will address one of the most important factors in your business - the workforce. At the forefront of your business are your staff and employees. Thus, apt care and attention are due to them, especially if you are keen on employing and maintaining the most dynamic, dependable, and skilled people. Global business strategy consulting firms can keep you abreast with the latest trends and practices in recruitment, compensations, benefits, perks, and other related information. Acquiring this kind of know-how will give you better chances of attracting a commendable and loyal workforce.

Business owners now have a competent, dependable, and efficient business partner in the form of international management consulting. This type of investment will surely reap you benefits which you otherwise would not be able to enjoy. Your global business strategy consulting partner can be depended on to keep your business' interests at heart.

Together, you can work towards a brighter, more stable future for your company.

Build A Global Business Online Using The Right Tools And The Right System

When starting out as an online internet marketer often times you will ask yourself who is my target audience? The usual common response is EVERYONE! As an internet marketer, you feel passionate about your product and you believe everyone will benefit from it, though that may be true to some extent, not everyone is interested in what you have to offer. Though you may think your target audience is 'everyone', you really should be saying my target audience is 'everywhere'. Internet marketing is not limited to local cities or regions or countries. Internet marketing is a global worldwide business. As an internet marketer, you need to look at your business as a true multi-continental business and that you can have clients and customers from anywhere in the world.

With the power of the internet and with the right tools and the right system you can reach anybody from anywhere in the world. That means you need to view your business as a global business. There are two critical things any business is going to need in becoming a global business;

✓The Right Tools, and

✓The Right System

The Right Tools:

There are certain internet marketing tools that one must have to be able to grow their business. There two main tools that are must-have, the first is known as a lead capture page or squeeze page. This page is what you need to send your potential clients too. If you have a compelling product or service they will want to know more about and want more information. This is where the lead capture page comes into place. These potential customers will "opt-in" by submitting their name and email. Guess what you now have a lead for a potential sale of your product, service or business. This person could be your neighbor or someone on the other side of the world. This has to do with marketing your business. Well now you have their email what do you do with it, well this leads me to our next tool, an auto-responder. An auto-responder is a service where it will automatically email your potential lead with emails that you have created for those leads. Let's face it if you had 10, 100, or 1000 people opt-in as a subscriber you don't have the time to email each lead individually, that's why you must have an auto-responder. This takes care of this process for you.

The Right System:

To be able to implement the right tools you need to have the right system in place. What I mean by that is, you need to have a service that offers these tools and ongoing training with video tutorials to help you with this process. Learning how to use these tools can take a long time and can be a very expensive lesson to learn by yourself, however, if you have a system in place you will be able to master these tools in a very short period of time. The right system must have a service that will help you understand and automate this process for you. The system should have a support system of other more experienced internet marketers that can mentor and coach you. The system is what is going to keep you motivated as an internet marketer and help progress your business by learning how to use the tools and having the right tools will help you accomplish your aim as a global business and help you achieve much success in the internet marketing business.

Conclusion

Starting and running a small business can be the best decision you may ever make. Having the facts in advance of that decision is critical to ensure that you are positioned for success. Once you fully vet your decision-making for starting your small business, the rewards is amazing.

Thank you again for downloading **How To Start A Small Business In 2020.** *I hope you have gotten adequate information, and this book was able to help you start a refutable offline or online business.*
Would you please leave me a product review? Product reviews are the most important thing for my little company, and it would really help me out and only takes a minute of your time. To do that, you can click this QR code ,

and next to the **<u>How To Start A Small Business In 2020</u>**, *you can click how many stars you wish to give me and then leave a quick review.*
Thank you so much, and God Bless you!
Peter Quac

I appreciate your commitment and would like to offer you a **FREE ebook**
"Top Small Business Ideas to Start".
Just register on the link below

Thanks again very much.

Made in the USA
Middletown, DE
17 December 2019